I wish to congratulate Shell Malaysia Trading Sdn Bhd for sponsoring this colourful and pictorial publication *"Kuala Lumpur: Minarets of old, visions of new"*. This book captures Kuala Lumpur's skyline and the city's bustling and pulsating rhythm which is apparent everywhere. It documents the country's amiable climate in which a diversity of races, cultural traditions and beliefs thrive, grow and prosper unimpeded.

Shell's decision to sponsor the book is both praiseworthy and exemplary. The company's generosity is matched only by the creative talents of the late Mr. Peter Chay whose painstaking work brought about this book on the nations capital which we can be proud to see on bookstands anywhere in the world.

DATUK SERI DR. MAHATHIR BIN MOHAMAD
Prime Minister Of Malaysia

I would like to express my appreciation to Shell Malaysia Trading Sdn Bhd for taking the initiative to sponsor this colourful publication *"Kuala Lumpur: Minarets of old, visions of new"*. It is indeed an exciting pictorial collection of Malaysian life depicting its richness in diversity which is so characteristic of Malaysia.

My congratulations also go to the publisher, Foto Technik Sdn Bhd and in particular, to the late Mr. Peter Chay in capturing Kuala Lumpur in such an attractive way. As 1990 is a "Visit Malaysia Year", I am most appreciative of this joint effort in helping us promote Kuala Lumpur in particular, and Malaysia in general, to tourists all over the world.

DATO' ELYAS BIN OMAR
Mayor of Kuala Lumpur
Malaysia

Shell is pleased to be the sole sponsor of this exciting publication *"Kuala Lumpur: Minarets of old, visions of new"*. 1989 marks a significant milestone in the national history, as it is the year Malaysia plays host to the Meeting of the Heads of Government of Commonwealth countries. It is with this in mind and to commemorate this historic occasion that Shell Malaysia Trading Sdn Bhd takes pride in sponsoring this book which illustrates the charm of the city of Kuala Lumpur where minarets of old jauntily co-exist with the modern multi-storey buildings and skyscrapers.

It is our sincere hope that *"Kuala Lumpur: Minarets of old, visions of new"* will create a greater awareness of our rich Malaysian heritage and attract more visitors to the shores.

DATO' JAFFAR INDOT
Managing Director
Shell Malaysia Trading Sdn Bhd

CONTENTS

Chapter 1

The Story Of Kuala Lumpur

The first decade

At a time when the great cities of the Western world were well into the age of industrialisation, when the Great White Queen Victoria sat brooding on her Imperial throne, one undiscovered valley just west of the Main Range on the Malay Peninsula lay quietly slumbering under the burning sun.

It had been so for hundreds of years before the mid-1800's, quietly green, even when commerce and conquests had made Malacca (Melaka), Penang (Pulau Pinang), and Singapore busy ports of call for the European powers.

But Klang Valley's turn would come with the irreversible actions of one man – Raja Abdullah – who was the cause of as much joy as sorrow to the people of his time.

Just "how" and "why" can only be answered if one travels back in time to when the valley was ruled by Sultan Mohamed (1826 – 1857) as the Sultan of Selangor, assisted by his court and territorial chiefs.

This third ruler of the State had made two losing ventures into tin mining in the Klang Valley and twice was bailed out by a Lukut – based tin miner and businessman, Raja Jumaat.

In return, the grateful Sultan made Raja Jumaat Chief of Lukut and gave a royal daughter as wife. If events had stopped here, perhaps Kuala Lumpur would never have been established. As it happened, the Sultan's action in 1854 was to bring devastating results 13 years later. Because Raja Sulaiman the Chief of Klang died that year, Raja Jumaat was able to persuade the Sultan to appoint his brother Raja Abdullah as the successor and thereby pass over the late Chief's son, Raja Mahadi, whose sense of injustice was to fester until it finally burst into rebellion in 1867.

However this was all still in the future and Raja Abdullah settled in as Chief of Klang and began to set his sights on how he could benefit from his position.

He was aware from the historical records of the 15th Century – perhaps even earlier – that tin exports had been an on-going venture from the Klang Valley for centuries. As territorial chief, he could exploit the deposits, the only question that needed answering was "how"?

(top) A general view of Kuala Lumpur in 1880. *(bottom)* Close up view of Kuala Lumpur in 1880.

His brother's influence again helped and Raja Abdullah was able to borrow $30,000 from Malacca businessmen to finance a prospecting party into the upper reaches of the Klang River. A party of 87 Chinese workers led by Raja Abdullah set out in 1857, poling upstream until they reached the confluence of the Klang and Gombak Rivers. On this spot dubbed 'Kuala Lumpur' or Muddy Rivermouth, the party landed and travelled into the area now known as Ampang, where indications of rich tin deposits were found.

Mining began after the surrounding jungle was cleared, but not for long. Malaria took its toll of 60 men out of the original 87. Fortunately, Raja Abdullah's brother in Lukut despatched another 150 workers and by 1859, the gamble paid off with the first export of tin.

So far, Raja Abdullah had triumphed over the odds. With commendable business acumen, he constructed godowns, shophouses and shelters which would not only facilitate tin export but would also be the base of supplies for its miners. These were located near where the party had landed in 1857 and was to become the core of the Kuala Lumpur of the future.

From this rough and tumble beginning, the mining town took root. The rumour of lucrative business – then as now – drew Malay, Chinese as well as Indian petty traders and Indonesians too, like an invisible magnet. Indian trade with the Malay Peninsula went back as far as the 7th century B.C., with traders from the Coromandel Coast of India being familiar visitors in settlements along the Malayan coastline. The rumour of money to be made merely accelerated Indian arrivals, helping to lay the foundation for the country's subsequent multi-racial composition.

The town in those early years was a ramshackle clutch of wooden buildings and attap huts. Each ethnic group had its own 'quarter' – the Malays settled in villages upstream from the confluence of the two rivers towards what is Bukit Nanas (Pineapple Hill) now. On this hill, which gave a sweeping panorama of the town below, the Malays built a fort for defence purposes. The Chinese, on the other hand, opted for convenience and confined themselves downstream to the areas around Jalan Bandar and Jalan Petaling as they are known today.

As the Chinese flocked into Kuala Lumpur, a system of representing their interests, welfare and wellbeing was evolved. With the consent of Raja Abdullah and the support of one of the early Sumatran businessmen by the name of Sutan Puasa, Hiu Siew was elected the first Kapitan China or headman. The second was Liu Ngim Kong who was in turn succeeded by the famous Yap Ah Loy from 1868 to 1885. Both Sutan and Yap were to feature largely in the second decade of the town's life.

The civil wars

The second decade was the time of the civil war in Selangor which erupted from 1867 and ended in 1873. Raja Mahadi who, 13 years earlier had been passed over as the rightful Chief of Klang, began the turbulence with an attack on Klang. Then he unseated Raja Abdullah, claiming the Chief's position for himself when Sultan Abdul Samad (the ruler then) made an objection. A retaliatory move by Raja Abdullah to retake Klang failed and he faded away to die in exile in Malacca.

In 1869, during a lull in the fighting, Raja Mahadi came to officiate at the installation of Yap Ah Loy as Kapitan China of Kuala Lumpur and to win his alliance. At the same time, the Sultan instructed his son-in-law Tunku Kudin to mediate in the fued.

Tunku Kudin's decision was to throw in his lot with Raja Ismail, the late Raja Abdullah's son, based on his assessment that injustice had been done to the Abdullah family. Secondly, Raja Mahadi had reneged on his promise to pay the Sultan a fixed income after the victory. As a result, Tunku Kudin recaptured Klang from Raja Mahadi who fled to Kuala Selangor. Yap Ah Loy, previously allied to Mahadi, changed sides after the victory.

But this was by no means the end of the civil war. There was still Kuala Lumpur.

In anticipation of an attack by Mahadi's allies, Tunku Kudin employed mercenaries to head the Kuala Lumpur garrison assisted by Yap's men. As expected, they were attacked in 1871 and over-run by Mahadi's forces, although Yap managed to escape to Klang where Tunku Kudin gave him asylum.

The tide of the war was to turn yet again, this time in favour of Tunku Kudin who, aided by the Sultan of Pahang's forces, managed to re-capture Kuala Lumpur. Raja Mahadi's allies, Syed Mashhor and the Sumatran Sutan Puasa, escaped the dragnet to find refuge in the remote areas of Ulu Langat and Ulu Selangor.

By 1873, it was all over. The Pahang forces withdrew to their bases while Tunku Kudin and Yap returned to a ruined Kuala Lumpur to begin the task of re-building.

After the trauma of the civil war, the third decade of Kuala Lumpur's life was to bring yet further changes caused by events in the state of Selangor.

The British factor

While the fires of the civil war were raging, the British Government in the Straits Settlements had been looking on with a growing sense of alarm. Particularly since incidents of such localised strife tended to occur in the other Malay states as well.

At heart, the British concern revolved around its self-interests. Rival European powers like the French and the Dutch were actively scrambling in the area for concessions that would help to broaden their spheres of influence. Given the in-fighting situation in the Malay states, the British were afraid that rival powers would seize the opportunity to interfere and take-over. Such a scenario would naturally curtail and circumscribe British activities.

It was against this backdrop that the British Governor of the Straits Settlements, Sir Andrew Clarke, probed for an opening that would lead to the Malay rulers accepting the appointment of British advisors or residents at their courts.

In the case of Selangor, the excuse was supplied by an alleged act of piracy by the Sultan's subjects on a British vessel while it was in his territory. The implication by the British was that the Sultan was unable to enforce law and order. Under the guise of helping to improve the administration and to maintain peace, the British edged the Ruler into accepting an Advisor whose role was advisory on all matters except those touching Malay custom and religion.

The acceptance of the Resident was tantamount to Selangor becoming a British protectorate with British officials automatically assuming a distinct status in the State. In fact, the officials were elevated to the prominence and power previously enjoyed by the Malay chiefs.

Despite his being a Kedah prince and therefore a 'foreigner', Tunku Kudin by virtue of being the Ruler's son-in-law was accepted by the local chiefs and rajas as Viceroy until the Sultan's young heir (Raja Musa) could assume power at his majority. But Tunku Kudin's vice-realty was shortlived – he relinquished the position in 1879 to return to Kedah.

In Kuala Lumpur, the effect of British protection was to stimulate its growth. The mines re-opened and the price of tin rose steadily as peace returned to the Valley. Besides tin, the country's agro economy also improved, more rubber plantations were opened in and around Kuala Lumpur and Indian labourers were imported to work in these estates, build bridges and roads. It was with the establishment of the British in Penang in 1786 that there began an influx of Indian sepoys who were ideal for maintaining law and order, building roads, bridges, harbours and reclaiming swamps.

Apart from these sepoys, another Indian migratory wave began in 1833 with the development of sugar and coffee estates in Penang and Province Wellesley. Indentured Tamil and Telugu labourers were brought en masse to work on these plantations, their numbers increasing from 1990 as rubber began to replace sugar and coffee cultivation in the estates.

The Malay and Chinese communities continued to live under their own leaders, separate yet in peace. And as a sign of the town's growing popularity, the new Resident Bloomfield moved his office from Klang to Kuala Lumpur in 1879, which from then on became the permanent location for successive Residents.

From 1880, there was no stopping Kuala Lumpur from becoming the burgeoning centre which finds its greatest expression today. A chronology of significant events from this year onwards testifies to its accelerated growth:

1880   : Kuala Lumpur is made of the capital of Selangor. Douglas Bloomfield the Resident initiates construction of government offices on the west bank of the Klang River, opposite the Chinese sector. The town then holds 220 houses of which 70 are Malay homes.

1881   : A fire from an opium shop spreads unimpeded, destroying nearly all the buildings. A flood at the same time devastates the tin mines.

| 1884 | : A volunteer fire brigade is formed with H.F. Bellamy, Public Works Department, as commander. Frank Swettenham, who replaces Bloomfield as Resident, directs re-building of the town with bricks and tiles. Road are also widened. |

1884 : A volunteer fire brigade is formed with H.F. Bellamy, Public Works Department, as commander. Frank Swettenham, who replaces Bloomfield as Resident, directs re-building of the town with bricks and tiles. Road are also widened.

1886 : A railway line connects Kuala Lumpur and Klang.

1888 : Alfred Venner, a planter from Ceylon, starts to convert a swampy ravine outside the town into a Botanical Garden. Now the Lake Gardens, the job took 10 years to complete.

1890 : King Chulalongkorn of Siam accompanied by the Sultan of Kedah pays an official visit of 3 weeks. Kuala Lumpur also gets its first English school.

1891 : In response to fears that rapid growth would reduce agricultural land in the town, 99 hectares for a Malay agricultural settlement are set aside. The area, called Kampong Baru, remains a Malay preserve even today.

1894 : The Secretariat Building opposite the Padang begins construction on plans drawn by the architect, A.C. Norman. It would become the administrative centre of the State for many years.

Victoria Institution is founded in response to growing demand for larger, better schools.

A factory is put up by the Public Works Department under C.E. Spooner to meet the growing demands for building materials. It is located near the present YMCA along Brickfields Road (Jalan Tun Sambanthan).

1896 : The Federated Malay States are formed comprising Pahang, Perak, Negri Sembilan and Selangor. Kuala Lumpur is the administrative centre because of its central location.

The first piped water from an impounding reservoir above Ampang is supplied to the town.

'The Malay Mail' prints its first edition of 200 copies in English language. The first daily newspaper, it was hand pressed in a Market Street shophouse, previously occupied by the General Post Office.

1898 : A town council called the Sanitary Board is formed to advise the Resident on day-to-day running of the town. Representatives from the various ethnic groups sit in and pass laws to improve social and health conditions for the people.

The last few years of the 19th. Century propelled Kuala Lumpur into even greater growth with the introduction of rubber into the country. Its successful cultivation brought a period of boom, one sign of which was the proliferation of schools being built to cater for the increasing numbers of children of all races. At about the same time, Port

Swetthenham was established as a major port which further enchanced Kuala Lumpur's primacy as a trading and commercial centre. When the 20th. Century dawned, the catalogue of development continued unabated.

1900 : The population numbers 30,000.

1903 : Kuala Lumpur hosts the conference of Malay Rulers of the Federated Malay States in a special dome-like structure at the Lake Gardens.

1909 : Masjid Jame, a replica of a North Indian mosque designed by A.B. Hubbock is built.

1910 : The railway Station from its North Indian pattern is built.

The population grows to 45,000 people.

1917 : The Railway Headquarters is built. Opposite the Railway Station, it is faithful to the style of architecture of its mate.

1921 : Town Planning Board is formed to develop the plan for designating different zones of the town into residential, commercial, industrial. The plan is completed by 1933.

1926 : One of the worst floods to hit Kuala Lumpur inundates many buildings. As a result, the banks of the Klang River are raised and its course straightened in those areas susceptible to floods, as an attempt to control future occurances.

1937 : The clock tower in Market Square is unveiled.

The Rubber Research Institute moves into its new premises at Ampang Road.

Plans are laid for a Coronation Park (the present Tunku Abdul Rahman Park).

1941 – 1945 : The Japanese occupy Malaya. It is a time of hardship for the people of Kuala Lumpur.

An error in Allied forces bombing in 1945 causes damage to the museum building and loss of some valuable artifacts.

1946 : British Military Administration, imposed at the end of World War Two, comes to an end.

The British introduce the Malayan Union, a form of government comprising the Malay States together with Malacca and Penang. As the Union denied traditional Malay supremacy over the other races, it was bitterly opposed. A mass Malay gathering in Kuala Lumpur protested against it and out of it is born UMNO, the Malay political party to safeguard Malay interests.

1948 : The Federation of Malaya is born and Kuala Lumpur becomes its capital, as it acquires municipality status.

| 1952 | : Petaling Jaya on the outskirts of the Kuala Lumpur municipality is chosen for development, and work begins. The events leading to its choice is the Emergency (1948 – 1960) which brought chaos and dislocation. Re-locating industries and squatters is the motivating factor. The first municipal elections are held in Kuala Lumpur. In 1955, the general elections are held in which the Alliance Party comprising UMNO (United Malays National Organization), MCA (Malayan Chinese Association) and MIC (Malayan Indian Congress) sweep the polls. Next phase: Independence. |

Onwards from the independence – Merdeka

With the successful push for independence achieved on August 31st, 1957, the country could finally shape its own destiny. And Kuala Lumpur from the onset took centre stage. It became the emotional rallying point for the reading of the Merdeka Declaration at the newly completed Merdeka Stadium, repeated in 1963 when Malaysia was born.

Following the decade of independence, a mood of euphoria was prevalent in the country. Kuala Lumpur was no less in the thick of things, expanding and developing ever faster, ever further afield. But one black day in May 1969 shattered the dream. This was the racial riots of May 13th. with Kuala Lumpur been worst affected. It took the Government and community leaders many painful months to diminish fears and unreason before life lapsed back into its easy-going fashion. Two years later, Kuala Lumpur experienced another trauma, this time through flooding. The 1971 flood was one of the worst in its history and damages was extensive to homes, buildings and the disruption of daily living.

On a happier note, Kuala Lumpur reached a milestone in 1972 when it was conferred City status by the Yang Dipertuan Agong (King). In 1974, it became a Federal Territory separate from the State of Selangor as benefits a national capital. This has been the added spur to development such that Kuala Lumpur today is light years away from the clutch of wooden huts that marked its birth. Instead, it is cosmopolitan in look with a melange of architectural designs that appeal to foreigner and local alike.

Admittedly, the story of Kuala Lumpur lacks the romance and antiquity of Malacca or Penang. But dynamism has fuelled its growth from Raja Abdullah onwards, and doggedness has brought it to triumph despite scarring events and its less-than-ideal geographic location. Certainly, it is a City that keeps proving that you can't take it for granted.

A general view of Kuala Lumpur in 1880.

(top left) Kuala Lumpur Railway Station in 1891.

(bottom left) The Selangor State Secretariat Building in 1896 (now known as the Sultan Abdul Samad Building). The building in the foreground is the Selangor Club.

(top right) Jalan Raja in 1900.

(bottom right) Old Market Square in 1900.

KUALA LUMPUR

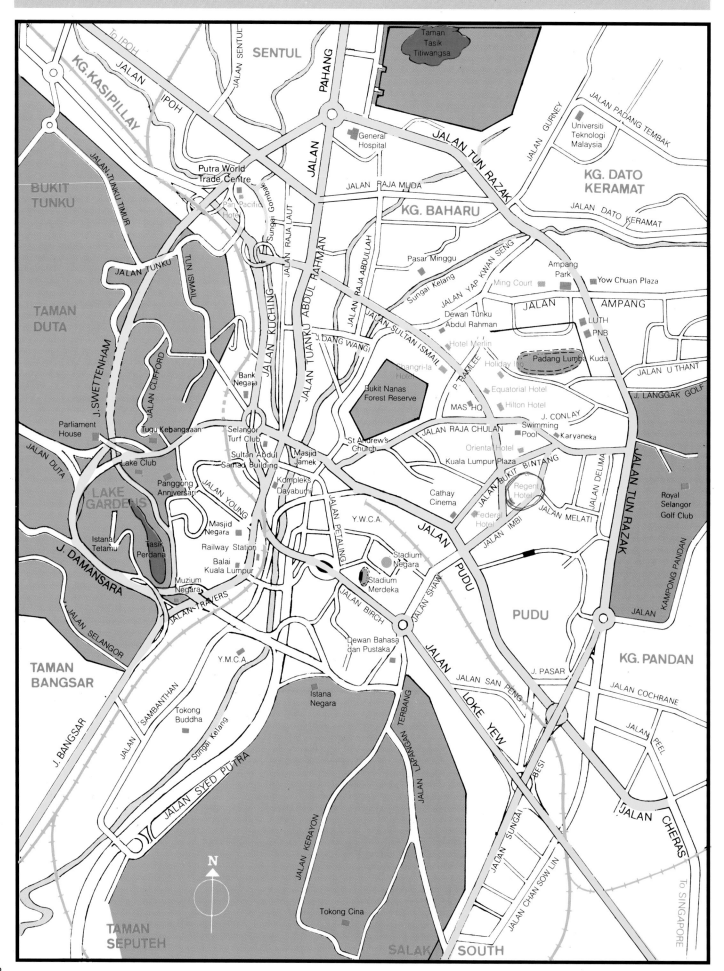

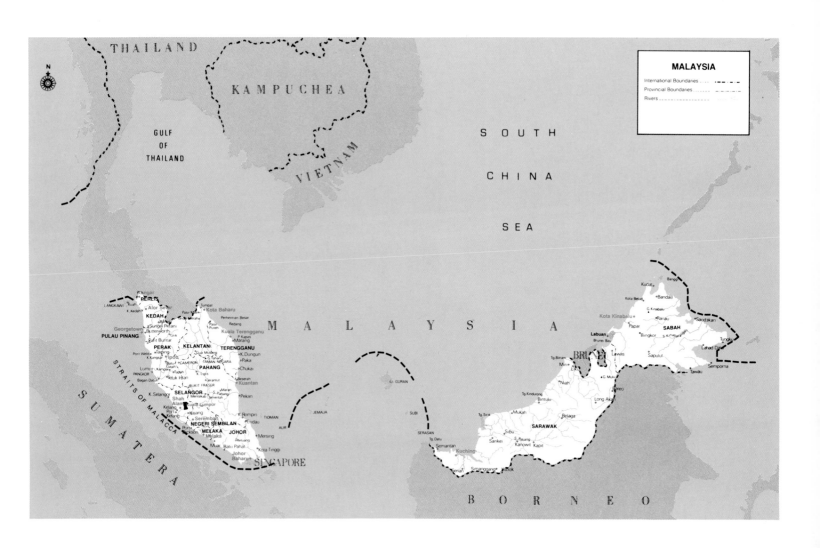

THAILAND

KAMPUCHEA

GULF
OF
THAILAND

VIETNAM

SOUTH

CHINA

SEA

N

MALAYSIA

International Boundaries ....
Provincial Boundaries ....
Rivers ....

SUMATERA

STRAITS OF MALACCA

PERLIS
LANGKAWI
Kangar
Alor Setar
K. Kedah
KEDAH
PULAU PINANG
Georgetown
Butterworth
Sungei Petani
Bukit Buntar
PERAK
Port Weld
Taiping
Lumut
K. Kangsar
Ipoh
Batu
CAMERON
Kampar
PANGKOR
Tapah
Teluk Intan
Bagan Datuk
K. Selangor
SELANGOR
Shah
Alam
Kuala Lumpur
Klang
Port
Kelang
Kajang
NEGERI SEMBILAN
Seremban
MELAKA
Melaka
Muar
Batu Pahat
Johor
Baharu
SINGAPORE

Jumpat
Kota Baharu
Pasir
Putih
Perhentian Besar
Redang
P. Kapas
Marang
Kuala Terengganu
TERENGGANU
K. Dungun
Paka
KELANTAN
Sungai Mudah
TAMAN NEGARA
K. Lipis
Temerloh
BUKIT FRASER
PAHANG
Jerantut
Mentakab
Maran
Beserah
Kuantan
Pekan
Gemas
JOHOR
Rompin
Endau
Mersing
Kota Tinggi
Kluang
Muar

JEMAJA

TIOMAN
AUR

P. GURAN

SUBI

SERASAN

MALAYSIA

SOUTH CHINA SEA

Kudat
Banggi
Kota Belud
Bandau
G. Kinabalu
Kota Kinabalu
Ranau
SABAH
Papar
Sandakan
Labuan
BRUNEI
Tg. Baram
Miri
Bengkor
Lahad Datu
Brunei Bay
Sapulut
Tawau
Semporna
Tg. Kindurong
Niah
G. Mulu
Long Akah
Bintulu
Mukak
Belaga
SARAWAK
Tg. Datu
Subu
Sibu
Bintang
Sarikei
Song
Kanowit
Kapit
Serian
Kuching
Simanggang
Lubok

BORNEO

19

Chapter 2

Kuala Lumpur Today

It has been said that the best way to get to know a country and its people is to plunge straight into its life, its streets, its activities. For the newcomer to Malaysia's capital city Kuala Lumpur, the following of this piece of advice can bewilder before it clarifies.

Almost immediately, a visitor will notice strange juxtapositions and the apparent lack of a single shaping spirit or unifying principle in the City. But with persistence and patience, most people discern an underlying pattern. One recurrent motif is a sort of bi-focal vision of the old and new.

Perhaps, a wag once ventured, this dualism could be attributed to the influence of the twin rivers, Gombak and Klang, that played such a vital role in the development of Kuala Lumpur. As if giving physical form to these forces, the City is indeed characterised by two 'streams' of architectural styles.

One 'stream' is represented by those monuments from the past – minarets of old, embellished at times with icing-like curlicues and spirals; copper-coloured cupolas perched on towers and turrets; Moorish-style arched doorways and windows; the odd Gothic or Tudor structure still sturdy, still functional. The second materialisations of "the new" comprises super-marvels of steel, glass and concrete typical of Manhattan or some mammoth North American city. It is within these modern citadels of power – often just round the corner or up a street from the jaunty edifices of the past – that the City's entrepreneurs, bankers, princes of commerce are hard at work to give concrete shape to their own visions.

But anyone who has ever visited or worked in this thriving metropolis would find it hard to imagine that this City did not even exist 130 years ago. Indeed, it is intriguing to wonder: what if in 1857 the first group of prospectors who came a-poling up to the confluence of the Gombak and Klang Rivers had **never** found the tin they were looking for? Or, what if all had perished of fever within the first month, instead of the 27 who survived?

However, it is known that Fortune smiled on this 'muddy confluence' (from which Kuala Lumpur derives its name) and that by 1870, the population numbered 2,000. From then on the little township was established, having experienced the usual baptism of fire that plagues most frontier settlements – gang wars, murders, fires and epidemics were rampant. It

3 Situated at the confluence of the Klang and Gombak rivers is Masjid Jame. Said to be built on the spot where Kuala Lumpur was born in 1857, this 77-year-old mosque was the city's main mosque before the National Mosque was built. It was restored in 1983 as one of the country's national heritage.

was the combined efforts of Yap Ah Loy (the famed Chinese Kapitan or Headman), Frank Swettenham (the first British Resident) and Tengku Kudin (the Kedah prince who was the son-in-law of Sultan Abdul Samad, the then Ruler of Selangor) that brought law and order.

By 1880 when the price of tin soared, a rich middle class was created. These newly minted tycoons built their magnificent villas along Jalan Ampang which remain today as exclusive now as then although few now remain since commercial enterprises and diplomatic missions have bought the plots and usually rebuilt in modern style.

In 1896, Kuala Lumpur replaced Klang as the State capital with a cosmoplitan population of 30,000 made up of Malays, Chinese and Indians.

Thus far, the history of Kuala Lumpur shows it triumphed over its accident of birth and the years leading up to the present indicate that there was no stopping the dynamo of growth. Kuala Lumpur today is home to 1.2 million people. It is also the seat of government; the political and administrative centre; the financial and business pivot; the location of the country's first university (established in 1959) and of more and more colleges; as well as the springboard to holiday spots around the country.

More interesting than this recounting of achievements is what the City is. Once adjusted to the bi-focal vision that KL (as it is affectionately known) imposes on the beholder, the old and new side-by-side no longer seem so bewildering.

In fact, that's the real appeal of KL, that haphazard throwing together of two disparate styles. The KL Railway Station, one of the best examples of Moorish architecture, has been sensibly preserved and maintained for its 'look' which both locals and visitors continue to capture with their cameras. Inside, though, it has been spruced up and gently modernised to make it as efficient as the spanking new trains that now move hundreds of people north and south daily.

Of the same period and genre as the Railway Station is the Sultan Abdul Samad Building with its copper cupolas and grandfatherly clock tower, and the two others beside it, the former Post Office and Public Works Department, (now Infokraf Centre). Across from these buildings stretches the *Padang*, the grassy parade ground for the annual Independence celebrations which was used throughout the year for cricket, hockey, rugger or rugby matches. Here, changes are afoot and this historic *Padang* will soon be converted into a Merdeka Square to commemorate the Country's struggle for "Independence". The English Tudor-style Royal Selangor Club frames the end of the *Padang* opposite the Sultan Abdul Samad Building. Fondly referred to as the "Spotted Dog" by habituees (because of a pair of dalmatians who were regularly walked on the grounds by their colonial mistress), the Selangor Club was erected in 1884 as the oasis for European social life. Today, clubbers sip their sodas in the leisurely manner of the earlier era, the environs much as they were when the club first threw open its doors.

These fine old buildings of a bygone era have continued functioning as originally intended. But there are other landmarks which, although outwardly the same, have undergone internal, functional changes. One of them is the Majestic Hotel opposite the Railway Station, once the elegant setting for parties and celebrations. It escaped demolition in the nick of time when the Antiquities Act came to its rescue, converting it into the National Art Gallery. Another is the original palatial home of Chua Cheng Bok complete with marble statuary with a Grecian cast which has been made over into the Le Coq D' or restaurant. But certainly more ambitious and laudable is the change that has come over the Central Market.

This squat, flat-topped building was designed in 1937 by Mr. T.Y. Lee, an engineer and architect with the then Kuala Lumpur Municipality. For almost 50 years this was where KL housewives came for their fresh meat, vegetables and fruits until the government decided the area should be re-developed. Following protests and the enthusiasm of a group of business-men who submitted an alternative to demolition, the Central Market was refurbished within and prettily painted in pastels without. Then lo and be-hold, it began life afresh as the centre for arts, crafts, food and games. To date, its success is unqualified as both a tourist 'must-see' and a place to browse for locals. And even though it may never yet rival London's Covent Garden (from which the planners drew inspiration), the Central Market stands as proof that KL people value the past as much as the present.

The present, of course, can never be ignored. But should a city be a mere replica of Manhattan, bristling with high-rises? Or should it make attempts to re-shape, re-interpret modernity, flavouring it lightly with its own cultural heritage?

Sensibly, architects of the second 'stream' have opted for the latter course and already the KL skyline is becoming a fine example of what a modern City can achieve if there is a concious attempt to blend old and new.

A stunningly modern landmark is the Dayabumi Complex, massively white but softened with lacy frills and arches that hark back to the past. Another is the LUTH building, its shape inspired by the 'rebana', a tradi-tional Malay drum. Yet it belongs to no other era but the present, given its vertically curved form which is acknowledged to be one of the rarest and most difficult shapes to build. Other examples abound throughout the City, most notable being new interpretations of the traditional Minangkabau roofs with their distinctive sweeping points. Overall, the im-pression of downtown KL is that it does not weary the eye with sameness – rather, here is variety where the old and new somehow balance, counterpoint and complement each other.

This seemingly odd pairing of past and present does not begin and end with the buildings themselves. Much of it is reflected in the way KL people live.

A neatly neck-tied and long-sleeved top-level executive can be equally at home in one of the swish, high-rise offices during the day. Then dance to a fenzied drum at any one of the leading discotheques or clubs after hours before rounding off the night in an unlikely place; hunkering down to a bowl of soup or noodles at a favourite open-air stall.

Equally commonplace is the sight of a modern housewife one moment pushing a trolley down a supermarket; then the next rummaging for bar-gains down Petaling Street, KL's Chinatown, before retreating up the

4 An aerial view of Kuala Lumpur in 1974. Besides the United Malayan Banking Corporation (UMBC) building (centre right) and the Bank Negara building (top right), they are hardly any modern high-rise buildings in the city at that time. The China town area with its 3 storey pre-war buildings is located on the right. In the foreground, the building with 2 yellow domes is the official residence of the King & Queen – *Yang Di-Pertuan Agong* and the *Raja Permaisuri Agong.* The early development of the city is centred along the Klang river. A prominent landmark on the out-skirt of the city is the Batu Caves *(top extreme right).*

5 (*following page*) The past 14 years have seen tremendous changes in Kuala Lumpur. The city of 1974 is a far cry from what it is today. Highways, flyovers – once a dream – are now a reality.

A mere 10 kilometres from the satelite town of Petaling Jaya, and about 50 kilometres from Port Klang, Kuala Lumpur is becoming one of the busiest cities in the South East Asian region.

The skyline is one of towering office blocks interspersed with trees. Contrasting these are old shophouses built early in the century that lend an old world charm missing from many modern cities.

The Daya Bumi Complex, the Islamic Centre (next to the National Mosque), the Menara Maybank (far right), the country's latest skyscraper, and the Putra World Trade Centre (top far right) stand out in the picture.

The sprawling green field (bottom right) is the Merdeka Stadium, with a seating capacity of 50,000. National and international level games are held here. It is also the site of the nation's Declaration of Independence in 1957, hence its name 'Merdeka (Independence) Stadium'.

A stone's throw away is the Chin Woo swimming pool. The city's green belt (top left), a popular recreational park, Tasik Perdana, remains relatively untouched by the past 12 years of development, and is highly popular as a jogging track and lovers's haunt.

6 Istana Negara, the official residence of Their Majesties, the Yang Dipertuan Agong and the Raja Permaisuri Agong, is a distinctive landmark in Kuala Lumpur on the way to the city. It stands on a 28 acres site.

Occupying a commanding position on the slope of a hill overlooking the Klang River, the Istana Negara was originally a double-storey mansion built in 1928 by a local millionaire Chang Wing.

During the Japanese Occupation between 1942 and 1945 it was used as a Japanese officers' mess. After the war, it was bought over by the Selangor Government for the Sultan of Selangor resident. It was later bought over by the Federal Government in late 1950s and converted into a King's Palace.

The first floor contains the private rooms of Their Majesties and two important chambers: The Throne Room and the Blue Room. The Throne Room in the West Wing is for formal occasions, while the Blue Room is the Audience Chamber where His Majesty receives Heads of State, Ambassadors and other V.I.Ps.

7 The Parliament House is the nation's symbol of democracy. Located on a hillock near the Lake Garden or Tasik Perdana, the building costing $16 million was officially opened in 1963. Dominating the complex is a 18-storey tower block which houses the offices of Ministers and Members of Parliament. The House of Representatives and the Senate are housed in a three storey block behind it. Located in the foreground is the National Monument.

32

8 9

8, 9 The National Monument is located on a five hectare site in Tasik Perdana, a short distance from Parliament House. It was set up in memory of the security forces who fell in the nation's struggle against communist terrorists during the Emergency (1948 – 1960).

The memorial comprises the Monument itself, a pool with fountains, a crescent-shaped pavilion, the cenotaph and the gardens.

The Monument proper of seven bronze figures, each three and a half times actual life size were cast in Italy. The statues were sculptured by Felix De Weldon, who created the famous Iwo Jima Memorial in Washington D.C.

10 On the fringe of the Lake Gardens or Taman Tasik Perdana stands the Muzium Negara (National Museum). Opened in 1963, it is on the site of the old Selangor Museum which was bombed in World War 2.

The museum enjoys the distinction of being the first-ever building in the City with a predominantly Malay architectural feature. Another point of interest are the two Italian glass mosaic murals that flank the entrance. On them are recounted the country's history and cultural activities.

Apart from permanent exhibits relating to the country's history, handicrafts, weapons, currency, flora and fauna, there are also exhibits from other museums and personal collections on display.

11 Circumcision, a young Malay man's rite of passage, is performed on male Muslims between six and sixteen years of age. Traditionally it is believed to be an effective way of upholding and maintaining cleanliness and good health.

In a royal circumcision, elaborate and colourful ceremony accompany the ritual. The last royal circumcision took place in Kelantan in 1933 with the young prince carried in a colourful procession; on arrival at the *istana* (palace) he was received by an attendant bearing a ceremonial yellow umbrella and a lady-in-waiting who scattered yellow rice on him. The prince rode on a giant model of a mythical bird during the procession.

The prince is escorted into a room where the *"mudin diraja"* (the person who performs a royal circumcision) awaits with two armed palace guards. The *"mudin diraja"* then performs the surgery in which the prepuce of the male organ is removed.

10   11

12 The National Mosque in Kuala Lumpur. The main dome of the mosque is designed in the shape of an 18-point star, representing the country's 13 States and the 5 Pillars of Islam. A 73 metre minaret, providing a platform for the muezzin to call the faithful to prayer, rises from a reflecting pool. The mausoleum located on the left foreground also has a reflecting pool surrounding it.

13 Muslims making their ablutions before performing their Friday prayers at Masjid Jamek. Because of its location in the heart of the city, this mosque is patronised by office workers and traders in the vicinity.

12   13

15   16   17

14 *(previous page)* The striking six-tier Thean Hou Temple perched atop the affluent residential area of Robson Heights, is not just a popular place of worship. It is also fast becoming an 'open air photo studio' among Chinese newly-weds who want an authentic Chinese backdrop for their wedding photographs.

One of the biggest Chinese temples in South East Asia, the M$7 million building is home to the Goddess Thean Hou, widely worshipped by the Hainanese community which emigrated to Malaya from Hainan decades ago.

15 The traditional Chinese temple has ornate and colourful carvings of dragons and a pagoda-like roof. Three main statues – the Thean Hou goddess, Kuan Yin (Goddess of Mercy) and Shui Wei (goddess of the Hokkien fishermen). Officially opened in November 1986, the temple has a few conference rooms and a multi-purpose hall.

16 Close-up view of one of the Goddess of Mercy (Kuan Yin). The Hainanese, mostly fishermen, worshipped the goddess as their patron saint. They looked upon the deity as their protector during long and dangerous fishing trips.

17 Offerings of food and Chinese Wine are made to appease the spirit who roam the earth during the seventh moon when the "hungry ghosts" leave hell for a spell.

41

18, 19 Sri Maha Mariamman Temple is the oldest Hindu temple in the city. The present structure was built in 1968, featuring the 'Raja Gopuram' or elaborate tower which is typical of South Indian temples. Ornate sculptures of scenes from Hindu mythology decorate it.

Hindu enter the temple barefoot and are required to wash their hands and feet at nearby taps in the temple courtyard before prayers, often burning camphor as an offering at the entrance. Priests, clad in white dhotis, conduct prayers called poojas, reading sacred verses in Sanskrit at the request of devotees. The devout Hindus prostrate themselves face downwards on the floor as a gesture of adoration. At the end of the poojas, they accept holy ash, sandalwood paste, vermilion powder, flowers and fruits from the priests.

Somewhat incongruously, this temple stands in the heart of Chinatown. In the early days the Indian pioneer, Thamboosamy Pillai, had asked for a plot of land to construct a temple from the then Kapitan China, Yap Ah Loy. The only available land at the time was the one where the present temple stands.

20 (following page) Southern view of Kuala Lumpur city with part of the Golden Triangle in the foreground. A regular feature are green belts interspering high-rise buildings. Bukit Nanas Forest Park is located right in the city centre, a patch of virgin forest that serves as an important air lung for the city. Recent urban development has resulted in a mix-and-mismatch of highly modern multi-storey buildings with old, worn out shophouses. In the mid-foreground modern high-rise buildings dominate the skyline in this highly developed sector. One of these is the office complex of Malaysian Airline System (MAS) symbolised by the red wau (Kelantan kite). Other corporations like Gentings, Promet and Malayan United Industries (MUI) are also located here. Strung along Jalan Sultan Ismail are major hotels like the Shangri-La, the K.L. Hilton, the Equatorial and the Merlin. The oval-shaped field in the immediate foreground is the Selangor Turf Club Race Course. This race course will soon be relocated outside the city and the present area will be developed into a recreation park.

18   19

21 Tasik Titiwangsa is the second lake-cum-park in the city. Opened in 1980, it is part of a government project to turn Kuala Lumpur into a garden city.

Once a disused mining pool and squatter area, the 44.5 hectare park, located off Jalan Kuantan, is now popular with picnickers and nature seekers.

Tennis and squash courts, a riding stable, a football field and an arena catering to remote control model car enthusiasts are available. Boat activities are also very popular at the lake, which is five times the size of Tasik Perdana.

Newly-weds posing in their wedding attire by the lake is fast becoming a common practice as the lake with the Klang Gate granite hills and the Main Range in the background makes a scenic background.

22 *(following page)* Kuala Lumpur, the garden city.

The city's green belt, Taman Tasik Perdana (foreground) occupies a 73 hectare site, housing two of the country's national symbols – the National Monument (far left) and Parliament House (not pictured).

The gardens, completed in the late 1890's, were initiated by Alfred Venning, a Ceylonese planter. He thought it was a good idea to have a garden as counterpoint to the hustle and bustle of city life.

Facing the National Monument is the prestigious Royal Lake Club, which was founded by 28 dissident members of the Royal Selangor Club in 1890. It is the doyen of all city clubs.

To the right is Tasik Perdana, encircled by a jogging track. Most of the roads weaving out of the trees and hills are closed to traffic to make the gardens safe for lovers of nature.

Some of the city's oldest trees can be found here.

21

23, 24, 25 A glimpse of the thousands of Malaysians from diverse cultural backgrounds who flock to the capital every year on Aug 31 for the National Day celebrations.

The parade, held in front of the Sultan Abdul Samad building, usually begins at around 7 a.m. Representatives of the people in their festive best can be seen stepping up to renew their pledges of loyalty to king and country.

Seen here are: participants from Sabah in their traditional costumes (**23**). Maidens in the baju kebaya, the national dress for women (**24**). School children of diverse ethnic origins are as one in their special T-Shirts (**25**).

23   24
25

33   34

33 A dim sea of light bulbs, scattered fires and in numerable pilgrims. Spent *kavadi* – carriers, free of their burdens, rest in the cool of the sacred cave and are ministered to by priests.

34 The chariot bearing the jewel-encrusted image of Lord Murugan is escorted in a procession by devotees on the return journey from Batu Caves. The $350,000 silver chariot is drawn by two garlanded bulls. All along the route, devotees break coconuts and offer prayers to invoke blessings from the deity.

35 *(previous page)* Calvary Church celebrated the birth of Christ with a four-night presentation of the "Singing Christmas Tree" using a hundred member choir. The singers took to the stage on a specially constructed platform shaped like a Christmas tree, decked with Christmas decorations and computer-controlled fairy lights which synchronised with the various Christmas songs.

36, 37, 38 Lion dances are usually performed during Chinese New Year, the opening of new businesses and other festive occasions to drive away spirit so that only good luck and prosperity remain. The beating of drums and cymbals provides the tempo for the skilful lion dancers. The lion dance usually culminates in the firing of fire-crackers.

39 The traditional Hindu wedding is an elaborate occasion. First, families of the bridal couple consult a Hindu priest who draws up horoscopes and sets a suitable date. Next, preparations begin. The wedding ceremony is usually conducted by a priest at a temple, a community hall, or at the home of the bride or groom where the bridal couple exchange garlands. The highlight of the ceremony is the tying of a 'thali' round the bride's neck by the groom, signifying the tying of the nuptial knot that binds the couple. At this point, all the guests shower the newly-weds with rice while throughout the ceremony, the priest chants Sanskrit Matras, bestowing God's blessings on the couple. This is followed by a grand feast.

40 A Malay bridal couple after their *bersanding* (tying the nuptial knot) ceremony, both attired in gold handwoven brocade or 'songket'. On the wedding day, the couple go through the *akad nikah* (marriage contract) ceremony, which is usually held in the morning. In the afternoon, at the *bersanding* the bridal couple sit on a colourful dais to receive the blessings of relatives and friends. A big feast follows the *bersanding*.

45, 46 A hand *batik* painting demonstration at Infokraf Malaysia, a local handicraft centre located at the former Public Works Department and Bank Pertanian Building. The Kelantanese and their East Coast counterparts are well-known for their colourful *batik*, a method of fabric printing using wax-resistant dyes introduced from Indonesia a few centuries ago. Whether hand-painted or stamp-blocked, *batiks* – ranging from dress lengths, sarongs to bed spreads, pillow cases and table-cloths – are popular with Malaysians of all walks of life and also tourists too.

47 A *kain songket* demonstration in the Central Market. A Malay lady sits behind a loom, turning fine silk and cotton threads into one of Kelantan's prized product – *kain songket*. This intricately-designed *songket* cloth has many varieties but is characterized by deep blue, green, maroon or purple silk shot through with silver and gold threads. *Kain songket* is usually used for formal functions, festive and special occasions, and also as evening wear.

45   46   47

48, 49, 50 Another popular tourist attraction is the Central Market. It sits on the bank of Klang River and is Malaysia's version of London's Covent Garden.

A mere two years ago mud and market garbage strewed the floor of this wet market, a far cry from what it is today.

The products on sale now vary from preserved nutmegs to brass candlesticks, from antiques to batik prints. You can also commission one of the many, young, budding artists clustering the two entrances to paint your portrait.

The original structure of the market was completed in 1886 and converted to the present one in the 1920s.

48   49
50

51, 52, 53 Dubbed the 'golden mile', Jalan Tuanku Abdul Rahman is a shopper's paradise. During the day, one can buy clothes, shoes and sports equipment; pewterware, antiques and household goods at the old shophouses and departmental stores lining this busy thoroughfare.

Between shopping, you can take in a movie at the Odeon Cinema or have a steak lunch at the old Coliseum Cafe.

Every Saturday evening, from 5 p.m. to midnight, a stretch of the road is transformed into one of the 86 night market sites in the city.

The 60 year old Jalan Tuanku Abdul Rahman previously known as Batu Road is ear-marked for further development into a pedestrian mall. This face-lift, to be undertaken by City Hall, will feature tree-lined spacious sidewalks and benches for shoppers to rest on.

51   52
53

58, 59, 60 Exotic Chinese, Indian and Malay food await the traveller at every street corner. Penang *Char Koay Teow* (58) is a favourite among locals and can be sampled at practically every Chinese eatery. The same can be said of *Koay Teow Teng* (59) and oyster omelette (60).

58   59   60

61 This satay seller with his tasty morsels of barbecued meat on bamboo skewers makes a good living in the City. Those in search of supper are often knowledgeable about where the best Campbell Road or Kajang satay are to be found.

62 A Roti Canai seller expertly twirls and tosses the piece of dough to a light, chewy texture before he fries it on a flat, round pan. Eaten with curries or on its own, a roti makes a hearty breakfast or snack for many Malaysians.

63 Here and there in the City can still be seen chendol sellers shaving ice by hand, using this wooden implement. The pot contains chendol, the green-coloured sweet noodles in a soup of coconut cream, delightfully delicious on a hot, steamy day.

61

62   63

64 Street lamps, car lights and a brightly lit fountain cut through the blackness of a KL night. Opposite the fountain is the old Town Hall, sitting at the corner of Jalan Tun Perak. Beyond it, not more than three hundred meters away, is the meeting point of the Gombak and Klang Rivers – the birthplace of the City.

65 More and more petrol stations stay open late in the night to serve the needs of the motorists. A familiar sight is this Shell Station in the heart of Kuala Lumpur which is open twenty-four hours a day.

66 At the top of busy Jalan Maharajalela near the Chinese Assembly Hall, this colourful fountain lights up the night. It's strategic location opposite the road to Stadium Negara and Stadium Merdeka ensures it gets the full attention of motorists.

64

65   66

70   71

70 David Copperfield, the renowned illusionist, staged his sell-out performances here at the Putra World Trade Centre. Completed in April 1986 in time for the PATA Conference, the Centre is a sophisticated, ultra-modern convention centre to rival the best in South East Asia.

Named after Malaysia's first Prime Minister, Tengku Abdul Rahman Putra Al-Haj, the Centre comprises the 41-storey Menara Datuk Onn tower block; the Dewan Merdeka; a 3500-seat plenary hall; the Dewan Tun Razak exhibition hall; two large conference halls; 13 meeting rooms as well as a full complement of meeting areas, shopping arcade, restaurants, banks and guest lounges. It also houses the headquarters of the United Malay National Organisation (UMNO) the largest component in the ruling coalition government.

71 The Dayabumi Complex, a fine example of modern Malaysian architectural form at its best, is strategically located on the bank of the Klang River. The complex comprises a 13-facet tower block and a podium.

72 Infokraf Malaysia previously housed the Public Works Department and Bank Pertanian. Prior to that, the building was originally constructed as Headquarters for the Federated Malay States Railway. Much later it was expanded to accommodate the Selangor Public Works Department. Along with this move, its facade was re-modeled to reflect the Moorish, Islamic-theme of the adjacent Government buildings. Today, local handicraft can be found on display and for sale at this centre.

73 Mahkamah Perusahaan or Industrial Court of Malaysia was established in 1940. This sturdy building again demonstrates the interesting details that distinguish the older buildings.

Historical Buildings

The real appeal of KL is the apparent haphazard throwing together of two disparate styles. The KL Railway Station, one of the best examples of Moorish architecture, has been sensibly preserved and maintained for its 'look' which both locals and visitors continue to capture with their cameras. Inside, though, it has been spruced up and gently modernised to make it as efficient as the modern trains that now move hundreds of people daily north and south.

Of the same period and genre as the Railway Station is the Sultan Abdul Samad Building with its copper cupolas and grandfatherly clock tower. Two others beside it, the former Post Office and Public Works Department, (now Infokraf Centre) are also tourist draws. While across from these buildings sprawls the *Padang*, the parade ground for the annual Independence celebrations and used throughout the year for cricket, hockey,

or rugby matches. Here, changes are afoot that this historic *Padang* will soon be converted into a Merdeka Square to commemorate the Country's struggle for Independence. The English Tudor-style Royal Selangor Club frames the end of the *Padang* opposite the Sultan Abdul Samad Building. Fondly referred to as the "Spotted Dog" by habituees (because of a pair of dalmatians who were regularly walked on the grounds by their colonial mistress), the Selangor Club was erected in 1884 as the oasis for European social life. Today, clubbers sip their sodas in the leisurely manner of the earlier era, the environs much as they were when the club first threw open its doors.

74

74 The Sultan Abdul Samad Building with its Moorish architecture and a 135 feet clock tower, has been a major landmark in the city. It was built from 1894 to 1897. Located near the confluence of the two rivers, Sungei Gombak and Sungei Klang, that gave Kuala Lumpur its name, it has housed the State Secretariat, the State Government Treasury, Federal Treasury, Attorney General's office, Accountant General's office and the Marriage Registry. Currently, the building after extensive renovations, houses the High Court and Supreme Court.

88   89

88 A *Silat* demonstration at a local hotel in KL. *Silat*, the Malay art of self-defence, was at one time an essential part of a young man's education. This art, believed to have been introduced to Melaka by a North Sumatran religious teacher in the early fifteenth century, is a popular pursuit in Kelantan. Students are taught by their *guru* (teacher) to parry any attack by opponents armed with a *keris* (double-edged dagger) or a sword. *Silat*, accompanied by rhythmic beats of gongs and drums, is usually performed during weddings and special ceremonies.

89 Kung-Fu, the Chinese martial art of self-defence. Two exponents of the art demonstrate their skill by bending two bamboo spears with their body without the spears piercing them and at the same time they could withstand the blows on their back by another two exponents using two sugar canes tied together. The canes broke into two on impact.

113

90, 91, 92 An adaptation of the *Gamelan*. Dancers hold fans to accentuate delicate hand movements. A variation of the Timang Burong, the dancers depict movements of the swallow. An orchestra of both male and female musicians provide musical accompaniment.

90 91
92

105 Tarian Rajang Beuh is a dance of the Bidayuh Community usually performed after the harvest season to entertain longhouse guests. The dancers' movements imitate those of eagles in flight. Male dancers sway to the rhythmic beat of drums and gongs and to the tiny bells on their ankles. They wear necklaces of wild boar teeth round their necks.

106 Ngajat Pahlawan is a battle dance or dance of the warriors. This dance involves two Iban warriors supposedly in armed conflict as they compete for status and recognition in the longhouse. In full battle attire, armed with a long sword and a colourful decorative shield, the warrior displays skill and agility. Occasionally he gives a battle cry to unnerve his opponent. The dance is a relic of the days when feuds were settled with the sword. Music for this dance is provided by a small and big gong, a drum, a tawak, bebendan and engkurumong.

105   106

107, 109 The 'Magunatip' Dance is popular among the Murut Kwijau of Bingkor in the division of Keningau. It is usually performed after the harvest season and as entertainment for guests. Magunatip is derived from the word 'atip' meaning 'sepit', which translated means "beat". In this dance, 4 seated dancers hold 4 bamboo poles forming a cross. As the poles are brought together and moved apart, 4 other dancers deftly step in and out to the rhythmic beat of gongs or tagunggak.

108 Daling-Daling, is a tribal dance of the Suluks in Semporna and Sandakan. Dancers sing verses to each other accompanied by the Gabang. It is usually performed at receptions and during festivals.

108
107   109

Chapter 3

Kuala Lumpur – Gateway To Malaysia

As the country's administrative, commercial and financial hub, Kuala Lumpur is the 'working capital' of Malaysia. But once the work is done by the week-end, during the many festive holidays occasioned by three religions and various state and federal celebrations or post-business conferences, local as well as foreign businessmen can often be seen heading out for a change of scene, a change of pace. In fact, with its network of roads, the City is the convenient springboard to east, west, north and south.

Within the state of Selangor, just outside the City's limits are a variety of attractions. Raja Abdullah's original storehouse (godown) is preserved in Klang, just 30 minutes west of the main airport. For the temple questing types, the developed suburb of Petaling Jaya yield interesting Siamese and Buddhist temples; Selayang to the north offers its famous Batu Caves with its 272 exhausting steps leading to the temple housing the statue of Lord Subramaniam; while in Shah Alam, the State capital, the Sultan Salahuddin Abdul Aziz Shah Mosque features a brilliant blue enamelled dome serene and yet vibrant in its technology.

For the less spiritually inclined, the alternative is to nip out to the Zoo at Ulu Klang for a picnic or walkabout. Or go a little further afield to Mimaland, that 120 hectare complex of swimming pool fed by a mountain stream, fishing lake, mini zoo, garden and rubber plantation all rolled into one. From here, it's not far to Genting Highlands – the casino in the sky – for a date with Lady Luck on the roulette wheel or to catch a spot of dazzling cabaret Las Vegas-style.

The slightly more adventurous may opt for Templer Park's 3,000 acres offering virgin jungle with well-marked tracks and Anak Takun Hill with its maze of caves and fossils. Because the Park is less than an hour's from the City and along the highway to Ipoh, it is ideal for those who want to see some real Malaysian jungle – without straying too far from civilisation.

Northwards from Selangor lies the 'silver' state of Perak, famous for its tin that for many decades, shared top billing with rubber as the country's most important commodities. The State capital, Ipoh, nestles in a valley surrounded by limestones hills that in two instances have become cave temples while in a third, pre-historic rock paintings have been discovered.

110 Shah Alam, the State capital of Selangor, is located about 16 miles from Kuala Lumpur, further down the Klang valley. "Shah Alam" means, literally, "King World". Artificial lakes, the hallmark of urban recreation, dominate the centre and dotted around the hillsides are several palaces and a sports club embodying the various styles of ancient Malay architecture. The enormous grand mosque, the Masjid Sultan Salahuddin Abdul Aziz Shah (foreground) provides the new town a focus for further growth. Its present population is about 80 thousand inhabitants.

But it is west of Ipoh, on the coast, that the state has truly taken off as a pleasure zone for fun in the sun. On Pangkor Island and Pangkor Laut, resort-style complexes have been built to introduce tourists to the emerald green waters. An added attraction is given to the coast with the Lumut Sea Festival that draws sea-sports loving crowds to cheer on the surfers, sailors and pillow-fighters on greasy poles.

Sitting on top of Perak is 'rice bowl' country – Kedah state and its tiny neighbour Perlis. Apart from this common denominator as the agrarian centres, Perlis has the additional advantage of being across the border from southern Thailand thus enjoying cultural enrichment and tourist dollars. Kedah is no less fortunate since the 99 islands of the Pulau Langkawi group which acquired free port status recently belong to it. These islands with their beautiful waters, romantic myths of White Crocodiles and tragic princesses are the stuff that dreams are made on. On the mainland, Kedah's appeal is that it is one of the oldest states as archaeological digs have confirmed. In the Bujang Valley, Hindu tomb-temples testify to an era of Hindu contact about 1,000 years ago.

South of the Langkawi Islands a rare 'pearl' tempts and tantalises the sun-worshipper. Here on Pulau Pinang, linked to the mainland by one of the world's ten longest bridges, the beaches with romantic names served by top-flight international hotels on the Ferringhi strip, are merely the prelude to the islands' seemingly endless charms. Tourist sights include the Kek Lok Si Temple with its Pagoda of 10,000 buddhas (count them!); a unique Snake Temple coiled about by Wagler's Pit Vipers rendered semi-comatose by heady incense; the Thai Wat with a 32 metre reclining Buddha; Pinang's oldest temple, the Kuan Ying Ting; the Kapitan Kling Mosque that's all dome and minaret; St. George's Church and the Cathedral of the Assumption; Fort Cornwallis built in 1808 to repel attacks; the funicular to Penang Hill; the Botanical Gardens crammed with plant life, macaques and waterfall.

But come December, the island is a veritable carnival with dragon boat races, float processions and *Chingay* derringdo – men balancing hefty 13-metre high bamboo poles on head, shoulder, stomach, chin or forehead. The atmosphere, already exciting, accelerates to fever pitch at this time and life is certainly a celebration on this Pearl of the Orient.

As the travellers zips along the East-West Highway to Kelantan, a sense of relaxation steals over him. For here is the perfect antidote for frazzled nerves acquired through City living: peace, quiet and deserted beaches. In Kelantan, life revolves around handicrafts which have always been revered. So wood-carving a palace or a salad server is carried out with loving care, while the makers of giant kites, tops and filigree silver jewellery, know no peers in the rest of the country. These traditions of cottage crafts and the still popular dance drama *(mak yong)* and 'shadow play' *(wayang kulit)* have helped to keep the cultural heritage of Malaysia alive.

The second East Coast state of Terengganu offers much the same idyllic scenery as Kelantan. But with an added attraction: that year after year, between May and September, an odyssey by the giant leatherback turtles culminates on the beaches around Rantau Abang. These half-ton creatures struggle out of the warm South China Sea waters in the dead of night to lay their hundreds of eggs, then slip back into the sea, not to re-appear until the following year. As part of the conservation programme, the leatherback turtle is now protected as an endangered species and the State Fisheries Department hatch and release the baby turtles from a percentage of the eggs collected. Apart from turtle-watching, Terengganu's off-shore coral islands like Pulau Redang and Pulau Kapas are great get-aways while *songket* fabric, brassware and woven-*pandanus* products are popular buys.

South from Terengganu, the main road hugs the coast revealing many miles of unspoilt beaches. It is here in the state of Pahang, just 47 km. from the capital Kuantan, that Malaysia's first Club Mediterranee at Cherating is located. Malay-style timber buildings dominate to give it a holiday village feeling. For those with more sophisticated tastes, Teluk Chempedak on the outskirts of Kuantan has a number of international class hotels as does the resort island of Pulau Tioman, about 4 hours from Mersing. But Pahang is not just sun and sand. Two hill resorts – Fraser's Hill and the Cameron Highlands which is on the Perak-Pahang border – are temperate zone escapes. The cooler temperature encourages tea plantations, roses, flowers and fruits while English-style cottages complete the picture postcard scenes.

Rugged adventures have also raved about the State's 4,300 sq. km. National Park with its big game attractions. The difference being the wild-life can only be 'shot' by the harmless camera.

A second refuge underway is the Endau-Rompin National Park which lies across Pahang and its neighbour state, Johor. This park of 84,000 hectares of tropical rainforest will be preserved against development to allow the rare Sumatran rhinocerous and other protected flora and fauna a chance to survive in their natural habitat.

Johor, by virtue of its being at the tip of the Peninsula, is also the land's end of mainland Asia. Across the 1,000 metre long Causeway lies the Republic of Singapore, for whom Johor is a welcome respite for reasonably priced fresh seafood, a weekend break at the beachside resort of Desaru or a picnic at the Kota Tinggi waterfall. Or perhaps a day trip to pick up ceramics at Ayer Hitam with a diversion to the impressive istanas or palaces of the royal family.

For a lesson in history, however, the state of Melaka is the rightful beginning. This cradle of the nation goes back to the 15th. Century and the town lives with its past on nearly every street corner. In the centre of the town, the distinctively red Dutch Stadthuys or Town Hall can be traced back to the 1640's while the Portuguese legacy of the formidable fortress A Famosa (built during their occupation 1511-1641) can only be glimpsed in the Porta De Santiago. The same is true of St. Paul's Church on St. Paul's Hill – bare walls and ruins. Bukit China and the Sultan's Well, both pre-dating these colonial relics, still stand with Bukit China acknowledged as the largest Chinese cemetery outside China with graves dating back to the Ming era. A private museum called the Baba Nyonya Heritage has been established in the town where intricately carved mother-of-pearl furniture and domestic artifacts can be viewed. This museum captures the essence of the sub-culture in Melaka shared with other centres of Straits-born Chinese whose 'form' is Malay in many ways but whose essence is Chinese, and whose imported artifacts are unique to this fusion of cultures.

Melaka has developed a tourist centre about 13 km. from the town centre. The Air Keroh Country Club and the Melaka Village Resort together provide accommodation, and a life-size collection of Malay village houses, a zoo and a crocodile park are the main draws for out-of-towners.

Within two hours' drive south from the City of KL lies another popular beachside playground, Port Dickson. The pride of the state of Negri Sembilan, PD's growth accelerated in the past decade due to its easy accessibility. Condominiums, hotels, time-share projects have erupted to give the town a 'little Waikiki' look.

No 'round trip' of Malaysia can be complete without springing from Port Klang by Feri Malaysia or aircraft to the Bornean states of Sarawak and Sabah.

Sarawak, famed for its colourful and noisy hornbills, is criss-crossed by rivers and generally presents a forested face. Nature rugged and primitive, is predominant which accounts for this state being a naturalist's haven. For here are limestone outcrops that are larger than life, craggier and more cavernous than anywhere else. Of the six national parks, Gunung Mulu is utterly impressive with outcrops stretching 40 kilometres. And beneath the peaks on these parks are networks of caves that include the Sarawak Chamber and Deer Cave, the former the world's largest and latter, the longest known. The Niah Caves also go down in history as being the site of the remains of the first South East Asian man, dating back 40,000 years. No less impressive are the ethnic communities that make up most of Sarawak's population. Their longhouses and unique traditional festivals add substantially to the 'richness' that is Sarawak.

In Sarawak, Malaysia's largest state, claims diversity for its memorability, then its neighbour Sabah must lay claim to having South East Asia's highest peak within its boundary. Mount Kinabalu at 4,101 metres is the focal point of its tourist attractions, where more than 800 species of orchids, 500 of birds and the world's largest flower (the *Rafflesia*) can be observed. Another naturalists' haven is the Sepilok Sanctuary near Sandakan where young stranded or orphaned *orang utan* are rehabilitated to regain their instincts of survival.

Malaysia's unique charm and significance to today's world is in its example of racial harmony and balance: a dynamic situation open to all pressures of politics and commercial development. Whether a resident of one of the nine Malay sultanates, whether originally belonging to one of the five historical Chinese mainland culture groups, or whether one of the varied tribes of Borneo or the hundred different language groups of India, every single Malaysian knows how to respect and live with its fellow citizens for everyone's mutual benefit – a lesson that the World must learn one day: and there is no better or more pleasant place to observe this wisdom than Kuala Lumpur.

111 Saujana Golf and Country Club, a comprehensive golf resort in the vicinity of the Subang International Airport. This resort comprises a hilltop clubhouse, two challenging 18-hole golf courses and the Hyatt Saujana Hotel and Country Club, an international standard 250-room hotel with a wide range of modern facilities.

112 Night view of the distinctive Kota Darul Ehsan Arch which marks the boundary between the Federal Territory and the state of Selangor Darul Ehsan.

This M$4 million marble arch re-states the neo-Moorish look of Kuala Lumpur's Railway Station, a landmark of the capital.

The arch sits astride six lanes of the Federal Highway with four century-old cannons retrieved from a fort in Kuala Selangor decorating the base.

113 Petaling Jaya, about 10 kilometres from Kuala Lumpur, has developed over the past 30 years from a squatter settlement of rickety huts to become Malaysia's biggest satellite town. Petaling Jaya residents now enjoy the highest per capital income in the city.

Travel between Petaling Jaya, the city (high-rise blocks in the distance), Klang and Shah Alam is a smooth and easy drive thanks largely to the Federal Highway.

Petaling Jaya's light industrial area (bottom right) is the source of tyres, soft drinks, electrical component parts, sweets and other consumer goods.

The prominent skyscraper is Menara Majlis Perbandaran Petaling Jaya (Petaling Jaya Town Board) built on the original site of a wet market.

112   113

114 The Masjid Sultan Salahuddin Abdul Aziz Shah is the newest and probably one of the most magnificent mosques in Malaysia. It is reputed to have the largest dome and the tallest minarets in the world, the dome is 92 metres high and its diameter is 51 metres; the minarets measuring 137 metres high. The M$162 million State mosque sits on a 15 hectare site next to an artificial lake in Shah Alam, the State capital. A striking feature of the huge blue and white dome, is the core panels which have Quramic inscriptions on them. The verses were written by Egypt's famous *'khatat'* (Quramic verses writer) Sheikh Abdel Monim Mohammed Ali el Sharkawi. Another interesting feature is that the dome itself is porus. Rain falls between the joints of the blue stove-enamelled outer panels and is collected around the impervious inner skin of the dome in a special channel. The water than flows down the main buttresses supporting the dome into a storage tank and it is pumped up into one of the four minarets. Worshippers making their ablutions before prayer trigger the flow of water from the tank by breaking a photo-electric beam.

The mosque can accommodate 17,500 people.

140

115 Pulau Angsa, just off the Kuala Selangor coast, is the only island resort in Selangor. Apart from a rest house, this idyllic island also has a lighthouse built in 1909 to guide ships in the Straits of Malacca.

116 A typical riverine fishing village on the west coast of Selangor.

115   116

117, 118 A majestic limestone outcrop located near the Selangor – Kuala Lumpur border. Within this gigantic rock mass is the fine network of caverns known as Batu Caves. The main Cathedral Cave with its huge stalactite that hangs about six metres down, houses the shrine of the Hindu deity, Lord Subramanium. Hindu devotees make a yearly pilgrimage here on the festival of Thaipusam, usually in late January or early February during the Tamil month *'Tai' 'Pusam'* is the star Pushyam which means "well-being". Hence, Thaipusam is the most auspicious Hindu festival.

119 A riverine fishing village on the Selangor River. Golden rays from the setting sun bathed the river turning it into a river of gold. Hurrying home with the day's catch is this lone boat.

120 Kuala Selangor, lying on the banks of the Selangor River about 64 kilometres north-west of Kuala Lumpur, is a peaceful and quiet place. Yet, it was here that many a bloody battle was fought between the British naval forces and the Bugis. This riverine town is also widely regarded as the birthplace of Selangor and was once the royal town of its early rulers. The relics of its rich historic past include the Kota Malawati (Fort Altingsburg), believed to be built during the reign of the second Sultan of Selangor (1778 – 1826), Batu Hampar (execution block) and the Seven Wells. The gleaming white lighthouse is the most prominent landmark and can be seen for kilometres around.

119   120

121 A bird's-eye view of Pangkor fishing village at Pulau Pangkor. The island lying off the Perak coast, is about 12 kilometres long and 4 kilometres wide. Pangkor town is the biggest of the three fishing villages located on the east coast facing the mainland of Peninsular Malaysia. The other two are Sungei Pinang Kecil and Sungei Pinang Besar just situated further up the coast. Historically, Pulau Pangkor was the venue for the signing of the Pangkor Treaty in 1874 on board a British warship anchored off the island which paved the way for the appointment of a British Resident in Perak.

Today, the island is being developed into a major beach resort.

122 An aerial view of the Penang Ferry Terminal at Georgetown, Pulau Pinang. The ferries ply the channel between the island and Seberang Prai or Province Wellesley on the mainland of Peninsular Malaysia. Georgetown, the State capital of Pulau Pinang is one of the Malaysia's main ports.

123 Pulau Pinang Bridge – the pride of the state – connects the island at Batu Uban to Seberang Jaya on the mainland. The 13.5km bridge, reputed to be one of the world's ten longest, was completed in 1985 at a cost of $800 million. It has a life span of over 400 years and is designed to withstand any earthquake up to 7.5 on the Richter scale. It has a four-lane carriageway with provision for expansion to six lanes. The middle span of the bridge has a 225-metre vertical clearance to allow ships with a maximum mast-height of 30 metres to pass. The bridge won the grand award for project design in the Consulting Engineers Council of Washington Engineering Excellence competition – the highest Washington State award – in 1986.

122   123

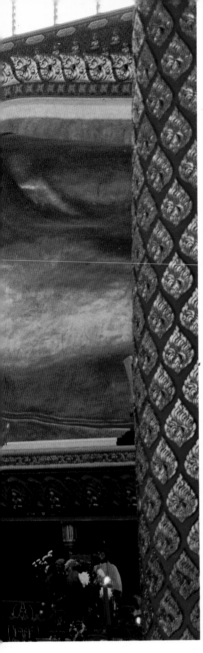

124   126

125

124, 125 The world's third largest statue is this Reclining Buddha measuring 32.4 metres. Located at the Thai Buddhist temple, Wat Chayamangkalaram, the figure is surrounded by smaller statues of the Buddha. Outside, fierce looking giants guard the temple entrances while immense naga serpents (mystical creatures that link earth to heaven) form balustrades at the doorways.

126 The Khoo Kongsi (*"Kongsi"* is a Chinese clan house or association for people with the same surname) was originally built in 1898. It was so elaborate that conservative clansmen warned that it might offend the Emperor of China. Mysteriously, the night after its completion, the roof caught fire. Clansmen saw this as an ill omen and rebuilt the house on a reduced scale. It is a treasure house with legends carved into the outer walls; giant guardian gods on the main doors with stone lions for protection; an altar of gold leaf and red lacquer; priceless statues and ancestral halls honouring the patron saints of the clan.

127 Under the Muda Irrigation Project, a dam on the upper reaches of the Muda River and a vast network of irrigation canals criss-crossing the Kedah Plain were constructed. This successful project together with the discovery of new paddy strains which can produce higher quality yield have resulted in a boom for local rice production in recent years.

128 Kelantan, well known for its handicrafts, shows its people take handcrafting seriously in this picture. For these fishing boats with their brightly coloured hulls and delicately sculpted sterns demonstrate that the Kelantanese just naturally include such cultural traditions into their everyday lives.

129 Everywhere you turn in this market place in Kota Bahru you'll see women in colourful headgear and clothes tending to their few square feet of space, piled with local produce. These shrewd queens of commerce have become such a dominant feature that their absence would probably be a big loss to the community.

130   131

130 The sea off the Terengganu coastline is a rich fishing ground. At the fishing village of Marang, fishermen spend the later part of their day mending their nets in readiness for the next morning's catch.

131 As the visitor drives along the 225 kilometers coastline of the east coast state of Terengganu, he passes by stalls set up by the Kampung folk. On sale are wares ranging from dried marine products to batek cloth. This Muslim girl, in typical Islamic dress for women, manages the family stall.

132 This stretch of beach at Rantau Abang, about 56 kilometres south of Kuala Terengganu, may appear desolate now but every year from May to September, it provides an almost perfect natural setting for Terengganu's greatest "performance" – giant leatherback turtles laying eggs. During this period, particularly the last two weeks of August, hundreds of thousands of visitors flock here and nearby beaches just to await the "stars" – the shy leatherbacks – in action. The best time to see this unique performance is at night, especially at high tide. All that is needed is a torchlight and plenty of patience. Local villagers usually patrol the beaches and alert the visitors as soon as a leatherback is sighted waddling up ashore. Rantau Abang is widely regarded as one of the world's prime turtle-watching territories. According to scientific studies, the beaches here have a very high rate of oxygen diffusion through the sand which is ideal for hatching. Situated here is a Turtle-Watching Information Centre which provides visitors a list of do's and don'ts of turtle-watching.

133 Natural artform ... these cluster of rocks lying just offshore of Kampung Kijal, a fishing village, resemble a man lying in the sea when viewed at a certain direction.

134 The giant leatherback turtle (*Dermochelys Coriacea*). This mammoth turtle, a primitive fossil-animal dating back 100 million years or more, is toothless and has powerful forelimbs like large flippers. Its back has seven longitudinal ridges and a mosaic of small bones covered over by smooth, leathery skin. Its weighs about half a ton and is almost 2.5 metres long.

133

132   134

144 Only 96 kilometres south of Kuala Lumpur is Port Dickson, the nearest stretch of beaches to the capital city. 'PD' as it is popularly known, is only 32 kilometres south of Seremban, the capital of Negeri Sembilan.

Port Dickson's proximity to Kuala Lumpur makes it very attractive to city folks as it is only 1 ½ hours drive away, compared to a four-hour road trip to the East Coast.

The attraction of Port Dickson is its 18 kilometres stretch of beaches ending in a head-land with a lighthouse dating back to the 16th century. Private holiday bungalows, condos, the Si-Rusa Inn and Ming Court Beach Hotel provide the holiday-makers' with comfortable accommodation.

Port Dickson residents are mainly small-scale traders and the pace of life is much slower compared to that of others seaside towns in Malaysia. Even the fishing industry is carried out on a considerably smaller scale compared with the East Coast.

145 Shell Port Dickson Refinery, founded in 1962, is today the most technologically advanced oil refinery in the country.

144   145

146, 147 Ibans account for about 30% of the total population in Sarawak and live mainly in the Second and Third Divisions. This male Iban in full ceremonial dress is about to perform the *Ngajat*, a Dayak Warrior dance, usually performed during the Gawai Dayak Festival to mark the end of a rich harvest. The headgear feathers are hornbill.

Ibans live in longhouses in the remote parts of Sarawak, fashioning them out of wood, bamboo, attap and propped on stilts. Longhouses are home to between 4 to 100 families with the interior divided into many units, each occupied by a family. Each unit has a bedroom and a kitchen and opens out into a *'ruai'* or large common verandah where residents gather for communal activities. Once head-hunters of Sarawak, the Ibans today cultivate hill padi and hunt in the jungle. They are a proud and resilient race, sharing a communal way of life, honouring the supernatural forces worshipped by their ancestors and remaining loyal to their heritage.

148 The river passage of Clearwater Cave, the longest cave in South-East Asia. So far, about 62 kilometres of this cave have been explored. The cave contains some of the world's finest underground rivers.

149 The Niah Caves, one of the world's largest caverns, is located in the centre of the Niah National Park. Evidence of man's existence from as early as 40,000 years ago has been found here. One of the caves known as the 'Painted Cave' was once used as a burial ground while rock paintings depicting burial boats are on cave walls. Millions of tiny swiftlets inhabit the Niah Caves, building nests with their saliva. These nests are the ingredient in birds' nest soup, a prized Chinese delicacy. The Caves are also the home of twelve species of bats. Guano, the excrement of the bats is collected and used as fertiliser.

148   149

The publisher is greatly indepted to Shell Malaysia Trading Sdn Bhd whose generous support and encouragement helped make the publication of this book possible.

The five guiding principles of the Nation known as the Rukunegara
have been formulated to bring about national unity to the multi-racial
people of Malaysia.

- Belief in God
- Loyalty to King and Country
- Upholding the Constitution
- Rule of Law
- Good Behaviour and Morality

To God be the glory for all that He has done.